Vin's Web

By Debbie Croft

Von sat at the bin.

She met Vin on the lid.

"Look at my wet legs!"
said Von.

"I am a bit wet, too!"
said Vin.

"Get up to my web,"
said Vin.

"Let us not get too wet."

But Vin and Von
can see Bud.

Bud has a big can.

"Bud looks bad!" said Vin.

"Run, Von, run!"

Vin and Von ran
to Vin's web.

"Run up, up, up!" said Vin.

"Let us sit in my
big web," said Vin.
"Bud can not get us!"

CHECKING FOR MEANING

1. Where did Von and Vin meet at the start of the story? *(Literal)*

2. Where do Von and Vin go to hide? *(Literal)*

3. What is Bud trying to do in the story? *(Inferential)*

EXTENDING VOCABULARY

web	The word *web* means lots of threads made by spiders to use as their home. What other names of animal homes can you think of?
looks	Find the base of *looks* in the book. What has been added to the base to make *looks*? How is the meaning of the two words different?
Vin's	Look at the word *Vin's*. What is the punctuation mark in this word called? Why is it there?

MOVING BEYOND THE TEXT

1. How many legs do spiders have? Can you think of any other animals with the same number of legs?

2. Are you scared of spiders? Why or why not?

3. Do you think Bud did the right thing in the story?

4. What should you do if you see a spider? Why?

SPEED SOUNDS

Kk	Ll	Vv	Qq	Ww
Dd	Jj	Oo	Gg	Uu
Cc	Bb	Rr	Ee	Ff	Hh	Nn
Mm	Ss	Aa	Pp	Ii	Tt

PRACTICE WORDS

Vin

Von

lid

web

wet

Let

legs